Unicorns

Printed and bound in Great Britain by
Hazell Watson & Viney Ltd, Aylesbury
for the Publishers, W. H. Allen & Co. Ltd,
44 Hill Street, London W1X 8LB

ISBN 0 491 02785 0

Unicorns

Edited by
Jeanne Griffiths

W. H. Allen · London
A Howard & Wyndham Company
1981

O here's the beast that no existence hath
By sight they knew it not yet held it dear –
Its roaming, bearing and its bray not wrath,
Even indeed the light of its soft leer.
Truly it never was. Yet though their love became
A taintless beast. For it, space ever freed.
And in that space, unhampered without claim,
Its head it nimbly raised with scarce a need
To be. They nourished it but not with corn,
But ever with the prospect, it might be,
And that gave so much vigor to the beast
That from its brow there sprouted out a horn,
One unique horn. To virgin blamelessly
It came – In silver mirror and in her to feast.

RAINER MARIA RILKE
SONNETS TO ORPHEUS

Father John:

The unicorns – what did the French monk tell me? – strength they meant, virginal strength, a rushing, lasting, tireless strength.

W. B. YEATS
THE UNICORN AND THE STARS

7

We caught the beast called Unicorn
That knows and loves a maiden best
And falls asleep upon her breast
We took from underneath his horn
The splendid male carbuncle stone
Sparkling against the white skull-bone.

WOLFRAM VON ESCHENBACH
PARSIVAL

All the beasts obeyed Noah when he admitted them into the ark. All but the unicorn. Confident of his own strength, he boasted 'I shall swim'. For forty days and forty nights the rains poured down and the oceans boiled as in a pot and all the heights were flooded. The birds of the air clung onto the ark and when the ark pitched they were all engulfed. But the unicorn kept on swimming. When, however, the birds emerged again they perched on his horn and he went under – and that is why there are no unicorns now.

UKRAINIAN FOLK TALE

The unicorn and I are one:
He also pauses in amaze
Before some maiden's magic gaze,
And while he wonders, is undone.
On some dear breast he slumbers deep
And Treason slays him in that sleep.
Just so have ended my Life's days;
So Love and my Lady lay me low.
My heart will not survive this blow.

LOVE SONG BY THE POET THIBAUT,
KING OF NAVARRE
13TH CENTURY

Unicornis qui & rinoceros
hanc haber naturam. pl
mal est simile hedo acerrim

13

Like a lion, without fear of the howling pack
Like a gust of wind, ne'er trapped in a snare,
Like a lotus blossom, ne'er sprinkled by water,
Like me, like a unicorn, in solitude roam.

HYMN OF BUDDHA

The unicorn has come out of the Forest
To graze the lush grass in the heat of the Sun.
All unaware of Passions arousing,
Oblivious to danger, in fear of no one.

Locked for her safety high in a turret
By Friends who keep a tight hold on the key.
A Princess yearns to be down in the Meadow,
To touch the moist muzzle longs feverishly.

Should she flee the Castle embrace the
    Unicorn
Garland the bright Horn with wild sweet
    flowers,
Run with hime back to the depths of the
    Woodland,
Risk their destruction by Men with cruel
    Powers.

No! leave hime to frolick alone in the Pasture,
Endure the hot longing of this summer day.
Disillusion's pain is not worth the Venture
Sweet lust and sad pining are endemic to May.

FRANCIS LUCIEN
ALLEGORIES

merum alerum n
nam quid desit m
hensurabiles posu
tantia mea tamqi

At this moment, the Unicorn sauntered by them with his hands in his pockets . . . when his eye happened to fall upon Alice: he turned round instantly, and stood for some time looking at her with an air of the deepest disgust.

'What-is-this?' he said at last.

'This is a child!' Haigha replied eagerly, coming in front of Alice to introduce her . . . 'We only found it today. It's as large as life and twice as natural!'

'I always thought they were fabulous monsters!' said the Unicorn. 'Is it alive?'

'It can talk,' said Haigha solemnly.

The Unicorn looked dreamily at Alice and then said 'Talk, child.'

Alice could not help her lips curling up into a smile as she began: 'Do you know, I always thought Unicorns were fabulous monsters, too? I never saw one alive before!'

'Well, now we have seen each other,' said the Unicorn, 'if you'll believe in me, I'll believe in you. Is that a bargain?'

LEWIS CARROLL
THROUGH THE LOOKING GLASS

The Lion and the Unicorn
Were fighting for the Crown
The Lion chased the Unicorn
All around the town.
Some gave them white bread
Some gave them brown,
Some gave them plum cake,
And drummed them out of town.

NURSERY RHYME

LABORA SUSTINENS

I saw there two and thirty unicorns. They are a cursed sort of creature much resembling a fine horse, unless it be that their heads are like a stag's, their feet like an elephant's, their tails like a white boar's, and out of each of their foreheads sprouts a sharp black horn, some six or seven feet long; commonly it dangles down like a turkey-cock's comb. When the unicorn has a mind to fight, or put it to any other use, what does he do but make it stand, and then it is as straight as the arrow.

RABELAIS
PANTAGRUEL

Unfetter'd by the world at rest,
Peaceful on the mother's breast,
By his artless trust betrayed,
In the trap her bosom made,
Such is the unicorn's arrest.

MISSAL AT NEUHASEN, GERMANY
ANON

O unicorn among the cedars
To whom no magic charm can lead us,
White childhood moving like a sigh
Through the green woods unharmed in thy
Sophisticated innocence
To call thy true love to the dance.

W. H. AUDEN
NEW YEAR LETTER

Will the unicorn be willing to serve thee, or abide by thy crib? Canst thou bind the unicorn with his hand in the furrow, or will he harrow the valleys after thou? Wilt thou trust him, because his strength is great, or wilt thou have thy labour to him? Wilt thou believe him, that he will bring home thy seed, and gather it into thy barn?

JOB 39 v.9–12

Take some unicorn liver, grind it up and mash it with egg yolks to make an ointment. Every type of leprosy is healed if treated frequently with this ointment.

Take some unicorn pelt, from it cut a belt and gird it round the body, thus averting attack by plague or fever. Make also some shoes from unicorn leather and wear them, thus assuming ever healthy feet, thighs and joints, nor will the plague ever attack those limbs.

Apart from that, nothing else of the unicorn is to be used medically.

ST HILDEGARD OF BINGEN
THE ROAD TO MYSTICISM

The shark is killed for its fin
The rhino is killed for its horn
The tiger is killed for its skin
What price the unicorn?

ANON

The unicorn, it's just been caught,
In maiden's lap, by cunning thought,
And – twas Jesus Christ!
O Mary, that's thy due,
And worth thou well hast earn'd
The stag with thee has sheltered,
Thou tender, pretty doe.

CHAPLAIN HEINRICH OF LAUFEBERG
A CHRISTMAS CAROL

Who shall hunt the Unicorn
Beast of myth and magic
Loved of woman rued of man
Endowed with power Alchemic

Deep within a forest lair
Blythely slipping every snare
Maid and beast entwined there
Sport in mists of fancie

We who hunt the Unicorn
Though it hath no earthly form
Scorn creations of the spirit
And it live we'll kill it.

ANON (17TH CENTURY)

Ioan. Collaert sculp.   Ioan. Galle excud.

There are wild elephants in the country, and numerous unicorns which are nearly as big.

MARCO POLO

In length each finger doth his next excell,
Each richly headed with a pearly shell
Richer than that faire pretious virtuos horne
That armes the forehead of the Unicorne

ROBERT HERRICK
THE DESCRIPCON OF A WOMAN

Like as a Lyon, whose imperiall powre
A prowd rebellious Vnicorne defies,
T'auoide the rash assault and wrathfull stowre
Of his fiers foe, him to a tree applies,
And when him running in full course he spies,
He slips aside; the whiles that furious beast
His precious horne, sought of his enimies,
Strikes in the stocke, ne thence can be releast,
But to the mighty victour yields a bounteous
    feast.

EDMUND SPENSER
THE FAERIE QUEENE

43

It is known that many kinds of animals not seen in other places breed therein . . . There is an ox, shaped like a stag, from the middle of whose forehead, between the ears, stands forth a single horn, taller and straighter than the horns we know.

JULIUS CAESAR
GALLIC WARS

45

I have seen in a place like a park adjoyning unto prester Iohn's Court, three score and seventeene unicornes and eliphants all alive at one time, and they were so tame that I have played with them as one would play with young lambes.

THE RARE AND MOST WONDERFUL THINGES
WHICH EDWARD WEBBE HAS SEEN

Then answer'd Percivale: 'And that I can,
Brother, and truly; since the living words
Of so great men as Lancelot and our King
Pass not from door to door and out again,
But sit within the house. O, when we reach'd
The City, our horses stumbling as they trode
On heaps of ruin, hornless unicorns,
Crack'd basilisks, and splinter'd cockatrices,
And shatter'd talbots, which had left the stones
Raw, that they fell from, brought us to the hall.

ALFRED LORD TENNYSON
THE HOLY GRAIL

49

The unicorn was white, with hoofs of silver and graceful horn of pearl. He stepped daintily over the heather, scarcely seeming to press it with his airy trot, and the wind made waves in his long mane which had been freshly combed. The glorious thing about him was his eye. There was a faint bluish furrow down each side of his nose, and this led up to the eye-sockets, and surrounded them in a pensive shade. The eyes, circled by this sad and beautiful darkness, were so sorrowful, lonely, gentle and nobly tragic, that they killed all other emotion except love.

T. H. WHITE
THE ONCE AND FUTURE KING

Now I will believe that there are unicorns

WILLIAM SHAKESPEARE
THE TEMPEST iii, 3

Illustration acknowledgements

For permission to use copyright material we are indebted to the following:

Rainer Maria Rilke *Sonnets to Orpheus* translated by J. B. Leishman, published by L. & V. Woolf, London 1936; W. B. Yeats *The Unicorn and the Stars*, Macmillan & Co., London 1922; Wolfram von Eschenbach *Parsival*, London 1894; Lewis Carroll *Through the Looking Glass*, Macmillan & Co., 1898; W. H. Auden 'New Year Letter', from *Shorter Collected Poems*, Faber and Faber Ltd; Alfred Lord Tennyson *The Holy Grail*, Strahan & Co., 1870; Edmund Spenser *The Faerie Queene*, Macmillan & Co., 1869; T. H. White *The Once and Future King*, Collins Ltd, 1958.